This paperback edition first published in 2015 by Delere Press LLP

Snapshots: a foreword © Lim Lee Ching
Layout © Chan Yin Wan
Text © Jeremy Fernando
Le Chapeau Invisibilité © Jachin Pousson

* * *

First published in 2015 by
Delere Press LLP
Block 370G Alexandra Road
#09-09 Singapore 159960
www.delerepress.com
Delere Press LLP Reg No. T11LL1061K

all rights reserved

ISBN 978-981-09-7903-4

Jeremy Fernando

For
The
Pleasure
of the Text
…

with a foreword by Lim Lee Ching,
Le Chapeau Invisibilité by Jachin
Pousson.

layout by Yanyun Chen

Snapshots: a foreword

We begin with the opening of the register, a register of writing.

Perhaps one that is overwhelmingly demanding. We begin by attempting to open with the register of writing.

Here, too, we find ourselves already attending to, attended by, the burdens of imposition. For how do we resist such a demand, how succumb to it?

At what point does our beginning *with* meet our beginning *by* to allow us to even *begin* approaching this opening of the register that is writing, the written?

Where, indeed, does it begin?

Oh, the audacity of this attempt.

Sir/Madam, we write to indicate our pleasure... we mean to say...to write...to text...To whom it may concern, we attempt to write to indicate our – that is to say, we mean to register our – interests in this, the possibility of approaching the, indeed this, beginning, this auspicious opening of the registers of meaning.

May the opening of registers ring triumphant!

We the undersigned...

Even here, when we say we, we are reminded that, between us and us, the text – a text, the texts – can be possible only because we are, in our lack of originality – our inability to begin, our lack of origins – nothing but a suspension of meanings, of unintentional clashings, like so many entangled wrestlers.

We meet this adversarial tension by confronting what it means to mean.

For to mean is to think, to attend to the implications of thought that, once expressed, escape us and persistently elude our attempts at reacquaintance. Thus, even as we continue to address the gesture of thought, it continues to haunt us, shape us. It taunts us, ever and ever with its suggestions of possibility.

And it is in this seduction that we lose sight of – miss, read – St Augustine's admonishments about not knowing for what we search, even as we find it. Truer words have never been written.

Nor read.

Except that this truth – all truths – must ever and already be unknowable, always snatched from our slippery grasps. Our words, our writing, our readings must ever and already be repelled by our very attempts to reach them, hold them out. The text thwarts its own efforts. The attempt is all.

How then, we remind ourselves, do we begin a book written about the death of the written – for we are still suspended in the throes of a difficult birth astride a welcoming grave.

The act of reading, the attempted resurrection of so many dead letters, can only truly commence by our surrendering to the denials, the textual shrouds that, in cloaking offer us the shape – the seductive, pleasure-giving figure of meaning – of the very thing they conceal.

Before we forget, the text reminds us that it is an artefact in flux; an artefact autonomous of its own creation; persistently an admission of its very constructedness, a constructedness that is both status and gesture. And in its constructedness, the text is held both in *stasis* and *kinesis*; delineated but infinite. It echoes, as Auden reminds us (and we misread) about poetry, in the valley of its own making.

Yet, it is this condition of undecidability that

allows it to *blend and clash*. The text must – will – always and already confess to – or be interrogated for – its complicity in its own contrivance, the demise of its own limitations in the pronouncement of its potentiality.

Perhaps we are never meant to know a text, never meant to enter its realm beyond the glimmer of suggestion it puts on. We must not claim possession, in turn cannot be possessed by it – trading the proprietary for the disappointment of propriety.

Even if some things cannot be had at any price, stakes can be claimed on the very limits with which we are faced as we prise kernel knowledge from the roots of refusal. And as it objects to us, so we take comfort in the echoes of possibility; the claims of knowing, of unknowing, resound with the truth of what we dream into knowledge.

The repetition is all.

For the text, the fiction that lay at the heart of each text, can only be realised by the re-affirmations that imagine it into its own narration; narrate it into our shared imagination. We are so many ancient mariners. We are ourselves so many penances.

Indeed, like the insistent intrusiveness at the heart of Coleridge's poem, a text at once demands our attention even as we feel compelled to cast our glance away. The text may not be a car crash but every act of reading is potentially a response to disaster, potentially a disaster unto itself. It consumes us, collapses the world surrounding us, overturns our expectations, reconstitutes our experiences. Reading does not merely re-write the text, it re-writes us as text. It adds to, remakes us, re-creates how we remember, what we imagine to be memories, re-calls the very language that utters us into meaning.

To that degree, reading effaces us at every and each opportunity. We are transformed by it. And because the text is everything and nothing, reading is simultaneously inclusion and exclusion, being absorbed, and being denied. We are perpetually confronted with the spectre of infinitude and void, helpless but for the necessity of responding to the great *may be*. We, the reader, are, in this, culpable for our own exception.

Which returns us to the attempt to write, to confront the impotence of inscription. For to write is to always be deterred by – and by the thought of – the murderous hand of reading. Yet, writing survives. It survives with determination, not merely because the act of creation is, in the disproportionate relationship between effort and effect, an act of violence, but because it plays the ruthlessness of reading at its own game: always seducing, always coaxing, always transforming.

Already promising.

Writing addresses an audience yet to be.
Writing is oblivious to the effaced reader;
it knows only the potential, thus potentially
infinite, reader. For we are legion.

Even as writing creates textual universes,
writing also assumes ecologies of – sources of –
experience.

Writing is premised upon and necessitated
by memory (remembrance, recollection). The
bonds between forgetting and remembering
may be latched on the dynamics and tensions
between past and present; always conditioned
by a sense of what is to come. But the creative
impulse will always be driven by the energies of
the imaginative return, the act of fabrication,
the weaving of the textual cloak that is made
possible only by the grace of repetition.

This collection, in committing itself to the
memory of Roland Barthes, attends to some
of the key aspects of commemoration, as
gesture and as intellectual tribute. It traces the
questions of what it means to mean; considers
the demands and possibilities of repetition;
and attempts to uncover, demythologise the
very act of text making. And if to mean is to
articulate, then the question of selectivity, hence

fictionality, must also be accounted for.

To read, to write, is to respond, to struggle for survival, to continually be compelled to a vigilance that will wake the dead. Indeed, the text is in the business of waking the dead – we can only misread anything into existence.

And if reading and writing demand choice, demand the vitality of response, demand the re-membering of the dismembered, then this collection can be seen as a petition for a re-examination of the death of the author.

Where do we sign?

Lim Lee Ching
March 2015
Singapore

Mirrors: no one has ever knowingly described you in your essence …
— Rainer Maria Rilke

Je serai ton miroir

…par Jeremy Fernando

Il a essayé de ne pas être vaniteux, mais il se contentait de l'idée de devenir célèbre.

— Silvina Ocampo

Il est assez difficile d'être assis, sur une chaise, pour regarder quelqu'un faire un croquis de toi. Regarder quelqu'un te regarder ; pendant qu'un croquis – peut-être de toi – apparaît sur une feuille de papier. Sur une feuille qui reste hors de vue ; qui se remplit au-delà de toi, est remplie de toi – alors qu'elle reste voilée de toi.

Marquée de toi.
Où chaque coup, ligne, trace, est une marque de toi.
Une marque qui ne marque rien d'autre que le fait que tu n'avais plus là. Que tu n'avais en fait jamais eu besoin d'être là.

Même si le site est de plus en plus rempli de toi.

Car tout croquis se fait à l'aveuglement.
Où, au moment où le coup est fait, l'artiste doit jeter un coup d'œil sur la feuille et non sur toi, soit sur toi et non sur l'espace qui se remplit de toi.
Un acte de mémoire ; toujours déjà hanté par l'oubli.
D'imagination ; la mémoire avec l'oubli qui est probablement écrit en elle.
En préparation pour rien d'autre que ton absence.

Préparation de ton absence – avec une autre.
Ou : préparer ton autre pour ton absence.

Un autre qui te regarde regarder.
Même si tu ne peux pas le voir.
Que tu sais – ou peut-être espères – qu'il te regarde en retour.

* * *

Portraits ;
traće (*traire*). Peut-être traîné,
tiré (*trahere*), en avant (*por*).
Trait, traîné.
Des lignes – rien d'autre que des traces,
traces (*tractus*).

Can the illegible be legible? If you want to read, jump, do not set yourself so much as a comma

— Hélène Cixous

Reading Jeremy Fernando

If writing is of the order of death, and reading of life — of reviving, resuscitation, perhaps even necromancy — the question that is opened is: *what happens in-between*? Or, perhaps more importantly, *what happens to the text in that in-between state*; where, when, it is neither alive nor dead? And as one attempts to bring the text from this death, does one have to — like Orpheus — just stare ahead as one reads; not look back lest the text fades away from one. Does one, can one only, read as an act of faith that something is coming along; that the text comes with us, from its grave?

Which opens the possibility that reading always also — if not already — entails a *looking away*, a turning of one's gaze, from the very thing that one purports to be reading, attending to, responding with. An averting of one's eyes at the very moment of reading. Which not only opens the register of reading as a moment of re-writing, but that this writing might not even be of the order of repetition. And, even if it is a

Reading Roland Barthes reading roland barthes

An encounter.

$$\text{The first line.}$$

A line before the first line in the text, the text proper.

> Perhaps then, an improper text — filled with impropriety. One that is speaking out of turn. Perhaps even *avant la lettre*. A text which always already runs the risk of being improper — thus, being excluded — evicted, no longer one's own (*propre*).

A line that appears again later in the text, but not in the same way: thus, a line that encounters us in this way, only once. Just sitting there, in an epigraph, much like a welcome, but perhaps also a frame.

repetition — for one also cannot write without repeating something, recalling a memory, harking back to language itself — it might well be a repetition of something completely other, of a completely different order, a repetition that depletes the memory of what it is purporting to recall.

Thus, reading is quite possibly a writing — even as that writing might well have naught to do with what is being read — even as one can only know of writing, if there is a writing, through reading, in the very moment that it is read.

And, in this moment of darkness about reading, what perhaps comes to light is the adage that *reading improves one's imagination*. Here, one should keep in mind that to imagine requires a certain correspondence; it has to be based on something previously known — in this case, language itself. Language that is based on other readings, other texts that one has read. Thus, there is a possibility that at the moment of reading — a moment that might always already remain shrouded from one — all that one is reading is every other text that one has read, every text except the one that one is attempting to read.

Thus, what is being raised from the dead is not so much the text that one is attempting to attend to, but every other text that one has read; the text in front of one being the ritual through

Tout ceci doit être considéré
comme dit par un personnage
de roman.

It must all be considered as if spoken by a character in a novel.

why 'as if' and not just a statement of :- this is a character in a novel'

clearly in remembering — a memoir — there is an imagining of who the person is . even of yourself.

but not just any arbitrary imagination — there has to be some (if not a lot) of knowledge . but just knowing is not enough . or is it that language always says more already . (cf: pp 48)

Roland Barthes - (n)either person (n)or character (n)either real (n)or imaginary . (cf: pp 44)

Roland Barthes. *Roland Barthes,* translated by Richard Howard. Berkeley: University of California Press, 1994: epigraph.

which reading takes place. But even as reading might be construed as a rite through which one passes in order to read and the text itself a sacrifice – not that we can fully comprehend what this even means – one should bear in mind Georges Bataille's teaching that

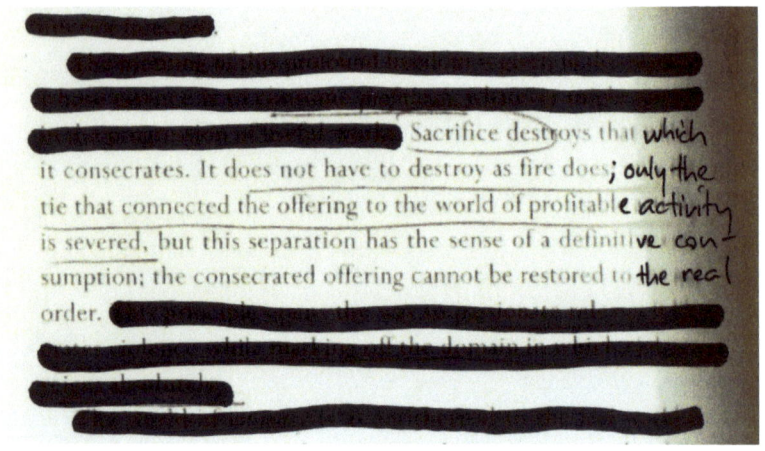

Sacrifice destroys that which it consecrates. It does not have to destroy as fire does; only the tie that connected the offering to the world of profitable activity is severed, but this separation has the sense of a definitive consumption; the consecrated offering cannot be restored to the real order.

Georges Bataille. *The Accursed Share, Vol 1*, translated by Robert Hurley. New York: Zone Books, 1991: 58.

Announcing a character called Roland Barthes – one whom he has named R.B. throughout his novel, perhaps even a nouvelle character in this novel that is ostensibly about himself. Though, the moment one writes about oneself is also the moment in which one has to step outside – whatever that might even begin to mean. Which perhaps open the question: is this step always the step beyond, also the not-beyond, *le pas au-delà?*

A question that might well remain beyond one, beyond us, perhaps only known to the one who attempts to take the step – perhaps only to Roland Barthes, if even so. And here, as I am attempting to read him, read Roland Barthes, it is difficult not to hear the voice of his friend, Michel Foucault, a soundless voice which continually resounds in me, a sound that voices:

> MICHEL FOUCAULT: *(long silence)* It's hard to say whether a book has been understood or misunderstood. Because, after all, perhaps the person who wrote the book is the one who misunderstood it.

Michel Foucault. 'The Gay Science', translated by Nicolae Morar & Daniel W. Smith. in *Critical Inquiry* 37 (Spring 2011): 385.

An utterance that could only be made after a

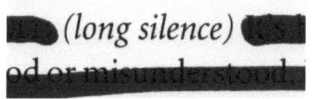

Ibid: 385.

And what is "severed" is precisely the notion of reading as production, of one gaining something from reading, of reading as "profitable activity."

In the attempt – for, it would not be a ritual if the end result was known, let alone guaranteed – to read, the text itself might well remain – after all, sacrifice "does not have to destroy as fire does" – but even as it remains, it "cannot be restored to the real order"; which suggests that the moment of reading introduces a cut, *caesura*, between what is being read and the possibility of reading. Which means that, not only does one quite possibly not know if one has read, one might not even know if one is reading. For, if it is no longer of the "real order" it is not only uncalculable, unexchangeable, but also beyond the *ratio*, rationality, beyond reason itself; perhaps also be beyond comprehension.

However, it is not as if one is unaltered by reading: that would be – or, at least, is potentially always already – untrue. So, what is perhaps also cut, "severed," "cannot be restored to the real order," is one's self.

Thus, one might well be changed, just in ways that might well be – remain – beyond one.

> But, in order to know that, one would have to attempt to read oneself.

— a silence that perhaps could only be admitted to in parenthesis. Perhaps an utterance that can only be made in the name of, through the name of, by naming another; by speaking in the third person: by an 'I' as "the person", as a character. Amplified by the silence: one stored for a long while, perhaps expanding in the, within its, parenthesis until it ruptures its boundaries, borders, frame.

A silence that might well be required in its naming, in Roland Barthes' naming it, as a "novel." For, once named — even if the name attempts to designate it so — can it, can anything, remain novel? After all, one must not forget that an act of naming — even if it is a creative act, an act of creation, a moment of bringing forth into the world, *tekhnē*, new-ness, as it were — is still premised on knowledge, on recollection, on memory.

>Always already in the past: thus, at best, a testimony.

However, here, one should try not to forget that every novel must act as if it is unaware of its own limits, its own finitude: it must be new to itself, new in its own telling of itself, as it were. The moment it testifies to its own fictionality, it no longer is so. For, the moment fiction testifies to itself as fictionality, it opens the possibility that its very status as fiction is fictional. That is, it opens the possibility that there is a truth in its

The text that is being read maintains its otherness from the reader (who is central) when the reader maintains a certain blindness to it. In other words, it is only when the reader does not claim full knowledge over the text but is in continual negotiation with it that the text remains fully other. It is the space, the gap, between the reader and the text that is the site of reading, for it is this gap that ensures that "understanding is [always] in want of understanding": the reader is responding to the text whilst acknowledging that it is impossible to fully understand the text, all the while realizing that understanding itself brings with it a non-understandability.[16]

It is this gap, between understanding and non-understandability, this gap within understanding itself, that ensures that reading can even begin to take place.

Jeremy Fernando. *Reading Blindly: Literature, Otherness, and the Possibility of an Ethical Reading.* New York: Cambria Press, 2009: 59.

fictiveness.

Which is not to say that even as it may be testifying to a certain truth that it manages to efface its fictiveness. For — as Jacques Derrida tells us —

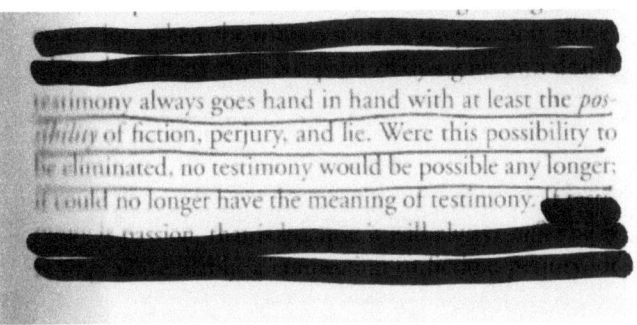

Jacques Derrida. *Demeure: Fiction and Testimony,* translated by Elizabeth Rottenberg. Stanford: Meridian, 2000: 27.

Which suggests that even as

Ibid: 30.

The risk perhaps of being literature.

than that, each eulogy is in preparation for the eventuality of our own absence.

Each writing, each inscription, is in some way in preparation for our absence: in future-memory of the eulogy that will be written for us—a call for that eulogy that is always already to come.

[This opens the register that every ti...

Jeremy Fernando. *Writing Death*, with an introduction by Avital Ronell. The Hague: Uitgeverij, 2011: 59.

And here, we should try not to forget that — as Georges Bataille reminds us —

). Literature, like the infringement of moral laws, is dangerous.

Georges Bataille. *Literature and Evil*, translated by Alastair Hamilton. London: Penguin Books, 2012: 17.

For,

Literature is not innocent. It is guilty and should admit itself so.

Ibid: 3.

However, one should bear in mind that literature does not quite exist without the one who attends to it, who reads it — and this might well be the very site of this danger, this evil which Bataille writes of, speaks of. An evil which, Paul de Man teaches us, begins with reading itself: for,

by the contemporary reader. Not that the act of reading is innocent, far from it. It is the starting point of all evil. "The woman who, in spite of the title, will dare to read one single page, is a lost woman

Paul de Man. *Allegories of Reading: Figural Language in Rousseau, Nietzsche, Rilke, and Proust*. New Haven: Yale University Press, 1979: 194.

The centrality of the reader.

The one who reads.

Without which, one is doing nothing but disavowing responsibility, denying that it is one — and no other — that is reading the text, making claims on and of the text, enacting a certain violence on the text.

Reading a text without recourse to — without turning to — the fiction of the one who has written it, the one who is called, named as, author of the text.

Without turning to the gaze of authority.

Without asking: *daddy, daddy, what is to be read?*.

Which also means that not only is reading an attempt to read in place of daddy — in the absence of daddy, perhaps even to exorcise daddy — but that, in the re-writing, one might well be authoring daddy.

In the reading, one might well be doing nothing but anointing oneself daddy.

But, even as literature, reading – reading literature – might be the "infringement of moral laws," a challenge, perhaps even evil, it also, at the same time, reinforces – perhaps even enframes – the very moral laws it attempts to undo.

> For, much like how the law assumes, needs, the criminal, the one who attempts to break the law – opposes, stands against, it – has to first assume its existence: thus, not only does the one who infringes quite possibly rely on the law, (s)he might well be the one who calls it into being.

Much like how all attempts at writing which infringes, that attempts to infringe, the laws of writing is hinged on nothing but grammar itself.

> For, grammar is "the system of relationships that generate the text and that functions independently of its referential meaning is its grammar. To the extent that a text is grammatical, it is a logical code or a machine. And there can be no agrammatical text, as the most nongrammatical of poets, Mallarme, was the first to acknowledge. Any nongrammatical text will always be read as a deviation from an assumed grammatical

Paul de Man. *Allegories of Reading* : 268

... in nomine Patris, et Filii, et Spiritus Sancti ...

But, even as one is doing so, this does not mean that one can fully exorcise the name that stands before one – the name of the author. The name that all attempts to read – even if reading is an attempt, one's attempt, "at responding to the text, whilst acknowledging that it is impossible to fully understand the text, all the while realizing that understanding itself brings with it a un-understandability" – are not only haunted by, but linked to, if not premised upon. For, even as one separates the text from the writer, the text does not exist without having first been written. So, even as one's reading of the text quite possibly happens independently of the one who writes it, the link cannot quite be completely severed. However, this is not a link that is based on intention – nothing quite so banal – but on the very notion that the text that is being read, the text that is being attended to, is the very same text that is written.

Perhaps, one might even go as far as to say: *reading is the moment when the text itself is authored* – by the one who reads – and *what is inscribed is the very notion of reading itself*. Never forgetting, trying never to forget, that

norm." However, de Man continues, for grammar to be conceived, all referentiality has to first be suspended; for, "just as no law can ever be written unless one suspends any consideration of applicability to a particular entity including, of course, oneself, grammatical logic can function only if its referential consequences are disregarded." But, for the law to be law, it has to have an applicability: thus, it comes into being, becomes, law in specific situations, within specificity. Hence, "it cannot be left hanging in the air, in the abstraction of its generality. Only by thus referring back to particular praxis can the justice of the law be tested, exactly as the justesse of any statement can only be tested by its referential verifiability, or by deviation from its verification." (Ibid: 269) This suggests that a text is both the result of grammar and is also its undoing; for both reading and writing requires the acknowledgment of, adherence even to grammar, even as literature itself might be the challenge to, an attempt to infringe, the law.

(Ibid: 269)

For, the infringement itself could not have been seen, known, felt even, without first the knowledge of grammar, the law.

writing, each moment of writing, is "in some way in preparation for our absence ... a call for that eulogy that is always already to come."

Thus, a calling for a text that is perhaps not quite there yet, but always already to come. A calling that never quite knows exactly what it is calling; a reading that never quite knows if it even is reading.

For, in every inscription – every writing by way of reading, writing that is reading – every *scribere*, there is always also the notion of *tearing*, *ripping*, perhaps even a mourning for what is unwritten, for the unwriteable in what is written ... written whilst *tearing*, with a small *tear*.

blind reading.

> Thus, grammar is — much like "moral laws" are — both the limit and condition of reading, writing, literature; perhaps even language itself.

And perhaps, this is precisely what remains novel:
>> for, the space between fiction and testimony opens the possibility that each reading is a witnessing of, bears witness to, fiction attempting to testify (to something, whatever that may be) even as testimony is narrating itself fictively. A relationality between fictive-testimony and testimonial-fiction in which the two remain perhaps not only indistinguishable but in

an infinite conversation

> A conversation that could well not-be without the witnessing.
> An encounter that only occurs as the witness is called to it, even as it is only called forth by the very act of witnessing itself.

Keeping in mind that,

> This is not a blindness that is negative in the sense of a deliberate refusal to see certain readings, certain possibilities, a blindness that is opposed to sight, but is rather a blindness that is inevitable, a blindness that is structural, beyond subjective choice. Not an "I do not want to see," but an "I cannot see":

Jeremy Fernando. *Reading Blindly*: 144-145.

Thus, just as

> scriptive relation; it is an act. The essence of testimony cannot necessarily be reduced to narration, that is, to descriptive, informative relations, to knowledge or to narrative; it is first a present act. When he testifies the martyr does not tell a story, he offers himself. He testifies to his

Jacques Derrida. *Demeure*: 38.

the essence of fiction, the narrative, the novel, also cannot be reduced to testimony.

Perhaps especially when one is writing about oneself.

Keeping in mind that as one is reading – even as this reading is fraught with blindness – that as one is attempting to respond to a text, a text that one might be writing as one is reading, one is also naming this very text as a text, perhaps the text, one is reading; one is naming it as one's text, even if that is a momentary naming. And in the moment of doing so, one is also inscribing the name of the author: this is why *the author is dead* – not because (s)he is not there, not because (s)he is missing, but that in attempting to read the text, one is always also writing her into being.

The author as the name for the moment, the site, even the possibility, of reading.

Keeping in mind that the one who writes is also the – her, his, one's own – first reader. For, there is no writing – at least, no writing that can be known – without reading. All whilst attempting not to forget Heraclitus' warning in his very first fragment – at least the fragment that we have deemed to be first, have named as first, that I have read as the first – that

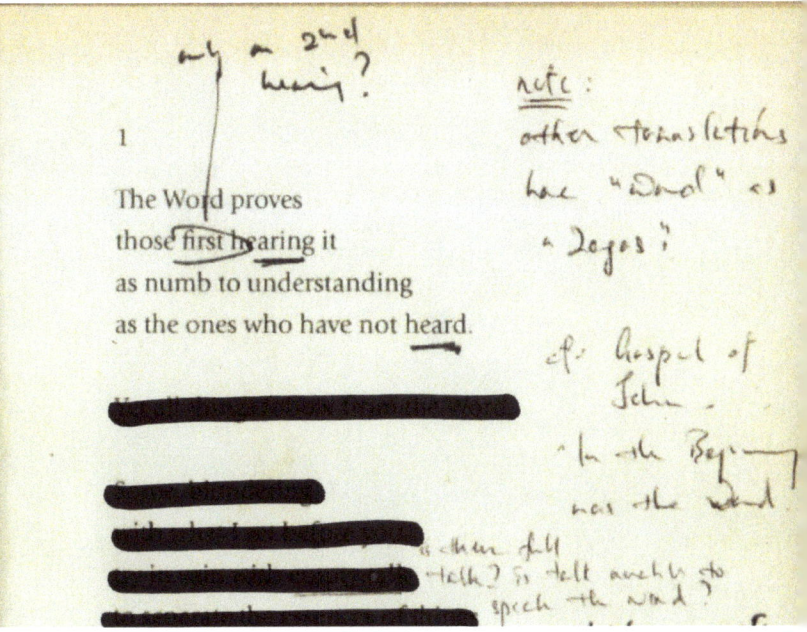

Heraclitus. *Fragments*, translated by Brooks Hatton. London: Penguin Classics, 2001: 3.

"Yet all things follow from the Word."

Reading as writing the author;
reading as a "call for that eulogy that is always already to come."

Even if one is the alleged author.

> Perhaps a silent following;
> perhaps a following only after a long silence.

A following that could only happen after the naming, after the naming of what is to be followed. A naming that occurs as if it could: after which, all that follows comes after, in succession. A following that always also brings with it – perhaps opens – the question: what comes before, what is before, what is the letter before it becomes a word, what comes before the letter, *qu'est-ce qui vient avant la lettre,* is there anything that can come before the letter, is the letter which summons, calls one, calls out to one, is one brought before the letter?

Perhaps especially when one is writing about oneself. But, as Elfride Jelinek might ask, "now who does the writer mean by himself?" Particularly in the moment – "now" – when (s)he is writing about herself, himself; one might even posit here, itself. Where not only is the self objectified as it is being represented, apprehended, spoken for, but that in its being written, it is the very object of the writing, perhaps of writing itself. Even as the writing, what is being written, might well come from the writer herself. For, Jelinek continues, "the writer goes forth from himself and then right away goes right away from himself, old and decrepit; he can only bring someone else to life, never revive himself." Ibid : 5

Elfriede Jelinek. Her Not All Her (or/with Robert Walser), translated by Damion Searls. Paris : Sylph Editions, 2012 : 5.

The Gay Science

Michel Foucault

Translated by Nicolae Morar and Daniel W. Smith

JEAN LE BITOUX: What is the reason that, of all your books, this first volume of *The History of Sexuality* is the one you think has been most misunderstood?

MICHEL FOUCAULT: *(long silence)* It's hard to say whether a book has been understood or misunderstood. Because, after all, perhaps the person who wrote the book is the one who misunderstood it. Because the reader would not be the one who understood or misunderstood it. I

Michel Foucault. 'The Gay Science', translated by Nicolae Morar & Daniel W. Smith. in *Critical Inquiry* 37 (Spring 2011): 385.

[redacted] ": I myself am my own symbol, I am the story which happens to me: *freewheeling* in language, I have nothing to compare myself to; and in this *move*ment, the pronoun of the imaginary, "I," is *im-pertinent*: *the sym*bolic becomes literally *immediate*: essential danger for *the life of* the subject: [redacted]

(This kind of embarrassment started, for him, very early; he strives to master it—for otherwise he would have to stop writing by reminding himself that it is language which is assertive, not he. An absurd remedy, everyone would surely agree, to add to each sentence some little phrase of uncertainty, as if anything that came out of language could make language tremble.)

Roland Barthes. *Roland Barthes*: 56, 48. italics from source.

For to understand, to claim comprehension, that one comprehends, is to seize, to grasp, to subsume a book under one, under one's self. It is to squeeze the life, the vitality, movement, out of the text.

But, it is not as if one can read without a gesture — no matter how temporary — of understanding. Even if one heeds Werner Hamacher's warning that

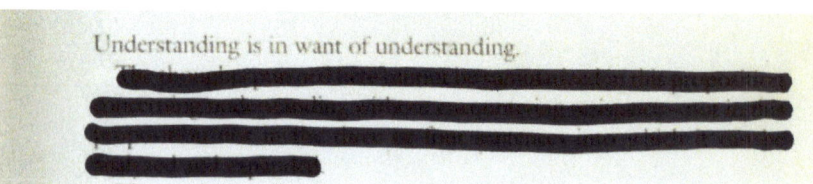

Werner Hamacher. "Premises" in *Premises: Essays in Philosophy & Literature from Kant to Celan*, translated by Peter Fenves. Stanford: Stanford University Press, 1999: 1.

that all understanding brings with it, is even premised on, un-understanding. That perhaps understanding itself is nothing more than a useful heuristic fiction; without which, however, no reading would be possible.

Perhaps then, the only one who can resist this gesture, this violence, this terror even — for it is not as if any permission was seeked, nor any attempt made at eliciting consent — is the one who writes. Not because (s)he is against murder,

An embarrassment that perhaps can only be admitted to, admissible through, within, a parenthesis; an aside (*para*) that nevertheless haunts, perhaps even displaces, the place (*tithenai*) that it tries to remain hidden from. And here, since the dossier of the inadmissible is opened, we might even attempt to sneak in — completely illegitimately — the notion of parentage in parenthesis. Not so much the notion of the father, of origins (*auctor*), from whom it — perhaps even R.B. — springs from, but the place from which it grows, is germinated, is brought into this world through. The place of the one who can "bring someone else to life";

mother.

From whom one is born.

Indisputably so.

For, the father, one's father, will always only remain a possibility, a probability at best. But one's mother: that is always already known — at least to her. Is absolutely singular. Which is not to say that one necessarily knows who one's mother is — let alone who she is. But that, unlike the father — who can only, at best, guess which might well by why he is the one who needs to authorise, even author, his claim over one — the mother always knows who came from, through, her.

but that (s)he has long already killed it; by writing it.

> [Perhaps this is why authors are sometimes valourised. For, as Michel Foucault teaches us:

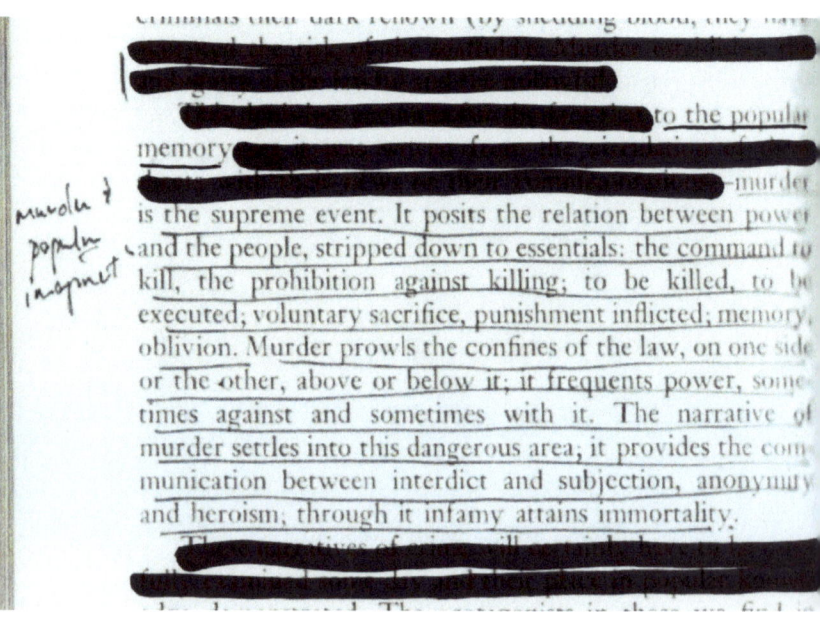

Michel Foucault. 'Tales of murder' in *I, Pierre Rivière, having slaughtered my mother, my sister, and my brother: A Case of Parricide in the 19th Century*, edited by Michel Foucault & translated by Frank Jellinek. Lincoln: University of Nebraska Press, 1982: 206.

> Mother
> Mother do you think they'll drop the bomb
> Mother do you think they'll like the song
> Mother do you think they'll try to break my balls
> Mother should I build a wall

Roger Waters. 'Mother' in *The Wall*. London: Harvest Records, 1979.

A text opened by an image of the narrator's mother, un-captioned, un-named, walking, perhaps strolling, sauntering – quite possibility not in any hurry, or least not that one, we, I, can see – towards the camera, towards the one who takes, captures, seizes, her photograph, her image. Quite perhaps unaware of the fact that she is being photographed: for, even as the eye of the camera sees her, her eyes remain shaded, veiled, from us. We see her, but remain blind to what she is, what she might be, seeing.

An image that is in full potentiality; a photograph with an absent object. For, unlike a painting, a photograph must have an object: and the image is, images are, written by light. So even as it might well be only a perspective, a particular testimony, there is a link, a relation, between what is written and what was before the lens.

A link usually framed – fairly or otherwise; perhaps always only, even already, a false accusation – by the caption, title, name that is given to the photograph: without which, the

Perhaps then, without this primordial murder, no act of writing would even be possible. Keeping in mind that what is being murdered is none other than the text itself. Not that the text dies, not that the one who writes even has a remote chance of killing the text — after all, it only comes into being through writing; thus, could not have been there, prior to any writing, to be killed — but that the attempted murder is the very ritual through which the possibility of writing is opened. Perhaps, *what is killed is none other than the one who writes*, the self who is attempting to write — at, in, the very moment of writing.

Which is why writing is "a call for that eulogy that is always already to come": for, it is nothing other than an attempted suicide.

image is left to float endlessly. Thus, even as there is no doubt that the photograph that opens the text is of a woman — we might even concede to it being the narrator's, *R.B.*'s mother — beyond that, nothing can be known.

> Hush now baby don't *you* cry
> Mamas gonna make all of your
> Nightmares come true
>
> Mamas gonna put all of her fears into you
> Mamas gonna keep you right here
> Under her wing
> She won't let you fly but she might let you sing
> Mama will keep baby cosy and warm
> Ooooh Babe Ooooh Babe Ooooh Babe
> Of course Mam'll help build the wall

Which opens another question: *what do we mean, could we perhaps mean, when we say that it was Roland Barthes who named the character R.B., that R.B. was born through Roland Barthes?* For, if the dossier of authorship is opened, and if Roland Barthes is the author of the name *R.B.*, then is he also its origin, its *auctor*? Which already quite possibly brings with it registers of fathering, fatherhood, echoes of Roland Barthes as daddy of *R.B.*. Along with — perhaps alongside — notions of authority, and the question of, *is Roland Barthes the one who authorises the character R.B., and perhaps even the text itself?* But here, we should try to bear in mind that authority is paradoxical:

Never forgetting – as Larry Rickels, channeling Freud, reminded me one summer in Saas Fee – that suicide is also an attempt at killing, murdering, the other.

1. Authority cannot be granted to oneself: in order for one to have authority, it has to be acknowledged by another. Moreover, this acknowledgement has to be granted freely; otherwise it would be a mere imposition of one upon another, a situation of terror and not authority. Thus, not only has there to be another, it has to be a relationship where both are wholly other to each other. Where, the other is the very condition of authority.

2. However, the very moment authority is granted to another, (s)he becomes an absolute other, unquestionable, unknowable. Daddy – to whom one can no longer speak with; where one is only spoken to. And thus, the very relationality that opens the possibility of authority – a relationality that is granted – is ruptured, shattered, by this act of authorisation.

Exercice scolaire ~ Academic exercise ~ *exercise?*

    1. Why does the author mention the date of this episode?
    2. How does the site justify "daydreaming" and "diversion"?
    3. How might the philosophy the author describes be "guilty"?
    4. Explain the metaphor "fabric."
    5. Cite the philosophies to which "preferentialism" might be opposed.
    6. Meanings of the words "revolution," "system," "image-repertoire," "inclination."
    7. Why does the author put certain words or expressions in italics?
    8. Characterize the author's style.

Ibid: 158.

And this is the true radicality of Roland Barthes' claim:

> 5. To know that one does not write for the other, to know that these things I am going to write will never cause me to be loved by the one I love (the other), to know that writing compensates for nothing, sublimates nothing, that it is precisely *there where you are not*—this is the beginning of writing.

Roland Barthes. *A Lover's Discourse: Fragments*, translated by Richard Howard. London: Vintage, 1982: 100.

Thus, the very moment when R.B. is written might well be the moment in which (s)he is completely separated from Roland Barthes; not necessarily, although it might well be, the person whom we call Roland Barthes, but the one who writes as Roland Barthes, who signs off as Roland Barthes.

To compound matters, at the end of writing – at the point where the writing is to be sent out into the world, as it were – one has to name oneself as author; write, put, one's name down. And at the very moment of doing so, at the very moment when one authors one's own name as author, one also undoes one's authority.

> And the text itself is perhaps emancipated from its author. Outside (*ex-*) the grip of the ownership (*mancipium*); away from the grip (*manus; hand*) of the one who owns, the one who takes (*capere*) control, who attempts to take control, call it, name the text, as one's own.

Where it is possible for Roland Barthes to write the text *Roland Barthes* precisely because it is no longer himself whom he is writing about; where it is no longer himself at the very moment he writes his name as the author of the text.

It is not just that one cannot write for another, for the other; it is not just that one attempts to write out of love for the unknowable, unreachable other, but that whenever one writes, one enacts a murder on the other – the other that is in one's self; the other that is the one who first reads what one writes, that brings one's writing into being through first reading it.

Not just that "this is the beginning of writing" but that *in the beginning there was writing*.

But not a writing of one, nor by an other, certainly not for another.

Just writing.

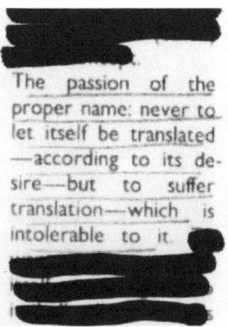

Jacques Derrida. *Glas*, translated by John P. Leavy Jr & Richard Rand.
Nebraska: University of Nebraska Press, 1990: 20.

Where perhaps writing about himself – about oneself – is always also the instant of one's – his – death?

And where '*Roland Barthes* par Roland Barthes' is always also '*Roland Barthes pour* Roland Barthes'; where in writing, inscribing, his own name, he is always also scratching it out, tearing the very paper on which he is attempting to write. Whilst perhaps always also crying out (*écrier*) as he writes *(écrire)*.

Writing as mourning.
A writing of mourning.
Mourning as writing.
Writing Death.

A death that he is perhaps attempting to stave off through the introduction of another name, a name in his place, a name which echoes – hints

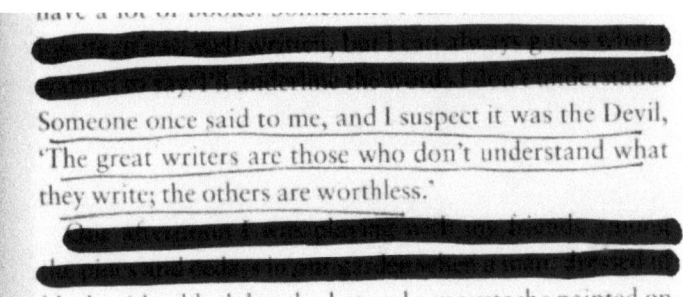

Silvina Ocampo. *The Topless Tower*, translated by James Womack. London: Hesperus Worldwide, 2010: 3.

[margin note: Perhaps only if it is a mystery, a secret.]

at – his own name, whilst never giving us the assurance that it is the same name. A name as perhaps a double name, a doubling of his name, even as we are never quite certain what is being doubled. Never forgetting – or, at least, trying not to forget – that, , each time he encounters one of these double words, R.B., on the contrary insists on keeping both meanings, as if one were winking at the other and as if the word's meaning were in that wink, so that *one and the same word*, in *one and the same sentence*, means at *one at the same time* two different things, and so that one delights, semantically, in the one by the other. Quite possibly even – keeping in mind that writing is only known at the moment in which it is read, that the writer is her own first reader – when (s)he encounters her own name. Which suggests that even as (s)he, the reader, Roland Barthes as reader, encounters *R.B.*, at least one of the possible meanings, possible references, of the name remains a potentiality, invisible to him, a secret from him.

[margin note: misterium tremendum]

And what is secret is nothing other than the name, his name, *R.B.*, itself.

For, a secret is not in its content but in its form: it is not enough to know the date of my birth, nor the digits that correspond to my naissance; one has to also know that they are the very numbers I use for my password; one has to know their significance before they have – and it is not clear if they ever have – signification, meaning.

One can, after all, only hope ...

And, since all attempts at knowing, at decoding, at knowledge itself, rely on meaning, schemas, heuristics — correspondence between an idea, thought, and something in the world — this suggests that even as one writes, even as (s)he writes her own name, her name as R.B., what is written remains, keeps itself, secret from him. Or, in his own words, every utterance of a writer (even the fiercest, the wildest) includes a secret operator, an unexpressed word, something like the silent morpheme of a category as primitive as negation or interrogation, whose meaning is: "And let that be known!" A meaning which is — says — nothing other than: there is something that is known; but nothing as to what that might be, could be, let alone is.

Roland Barthes. Roland Barthes. 72.

And, all that is known, that can be known, that remains to be known — quite possibly all that remains — is that her, his, my, name is *R.B.*.

A moment in which reading and writing collide; not only because writing comes into being the moment it is read, nor that without writing there can be no reading, but that without referentiality — at least no necessary referent — *R.B.* is the very point when reading and writing are in full potentiality. Where *R.B.* is a mark; one that is read, can only be read, as nothing other than a mark. A mark that marks; what it marks though remains hidden from us, from one, perhaps even from the one who writes.

Ibid: 145.

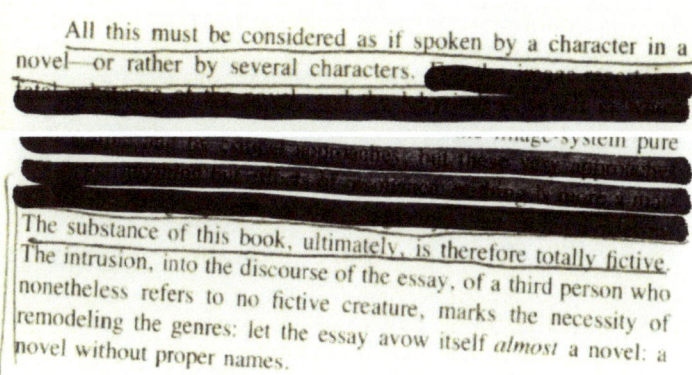

Ibid: 119, 120.

Which might be why *R.B.* admits within the text – but only within, boxed up, perhaps even away from the main text, almost aside, almost a side, *para*, text – that the actual title of the text is neither '*Roland Barthes* by Roland Barthes', nor 'Roland Barthes by *Roland Barthes*' (as both titles rely on the presence of an external referent) but *Roland Barthes by Roland Barthes*. For, it is an admission, it is only admissible, within, or aside: not because there is any greater truth within a space, between a space, or any such thing, but that it is something that could only have been uttered, written, by the one who is written, by *R.B.*, by the one who remains decidedly undecideable.

It always comes down to this: what is the project of writing which will present, not the best pretense, but simply an *undecidable pretense*

Ibid: 121.

[redacted]

[redacted]

writing 'this August 6' in September 3 ?
~ a reawakenment? a memory?

reading the corpus (
"do this in me
of me"

To write the body.
Neither the skin, nor the muscles, nor the bones
nor the nerves, but the rest: an awkward, fibrou
shaggy, raveled thing, a clown's coat

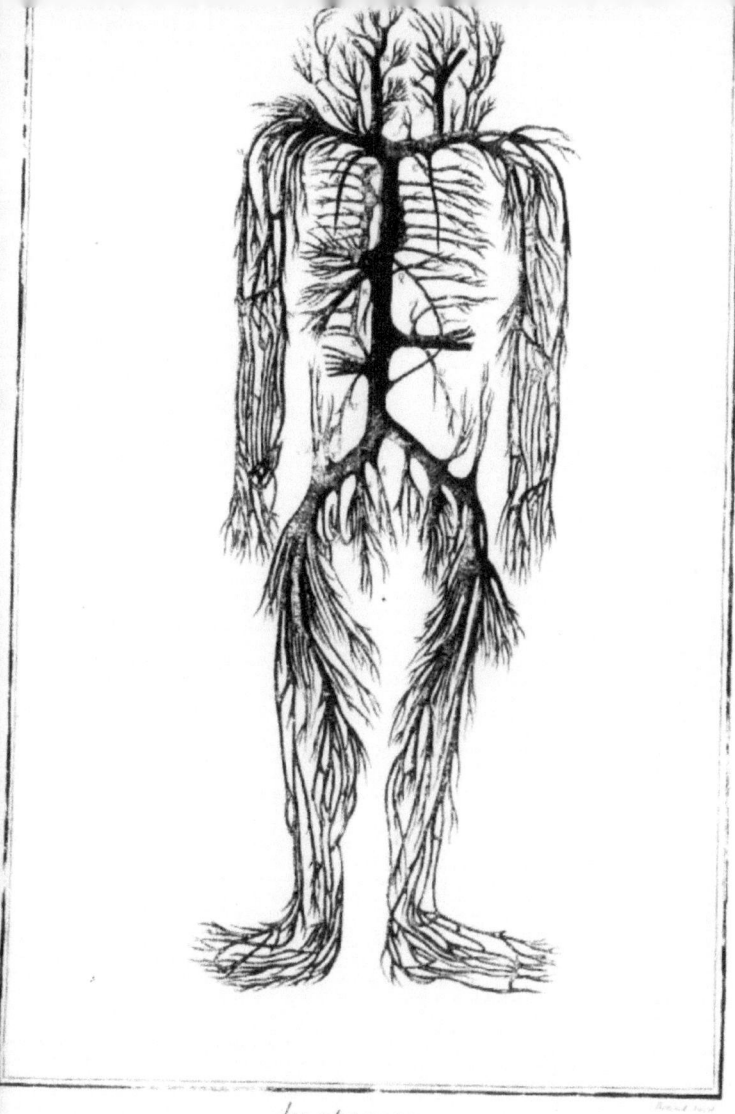

Anatomie

Ibid: 180.

"the rest": what remains.

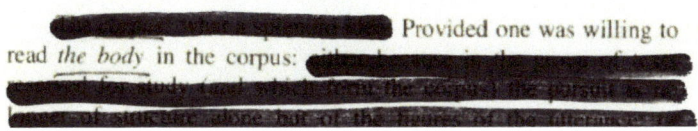
Provided one was willing to read *the body* in the corpus:

Ibid: 161.

In the texts.

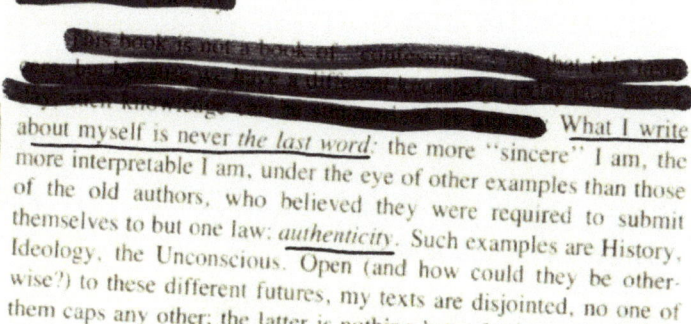
What I write about myself is never *the last word*: the more "sincere" I am, the more interpretable I am, under the eye of other examples than those of the old authors, who believed they were required to submit themselves to but one law: *authenticity*. Such examples are History, Ideology, the Unconscious. Open (and how could they be otherwise?) to these different futures, my texts are disjointed, no one of them caps any other; the latter is nothing but a *further* text, the last of the series, not the ultimate in meaning: *text upon text*, which never illuminates anything.

Ibid: 120.

* * *

the attempt to elucidate Blake through Jung tells us more about Jung's theories than about Blake's ▓▓▓▓▓▓▓▓▓▓▓▓▓▓▓▓ ▓▓ ▓▓▓ ▓▓▓. It seems to me that analysis is merely cancelling out a remarkable work and that it is substituting a somnolent heaviness for awakenness. ▓▓ For when we read Blake we hope that the world will not be reduced to those closed categories in which everything has been played out in advance, in which there is no quest, no agitation, no awakening, in which all we can do is to follow the track, sleep and breathe in time to the universal clock of sleep.

Georges Bataille. 'William Blake' in *Literature & Evil*, translated by Alaistair Hamilton. London: Penguin Books, 2012: 72-73.

The tygers of wrath are wiser
than the horses of instruction.

William Blake

For, when one reads, one

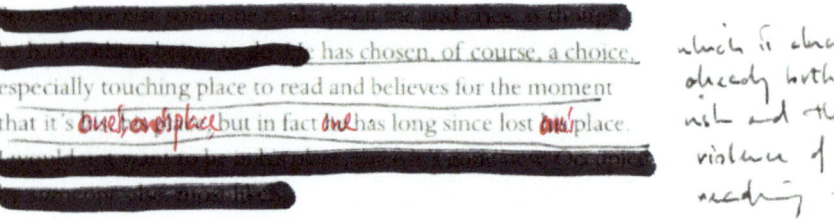

has chosen, of course, a choice, especially touching place to read and believes for the moment that it's ~~one~~ ~~and~~ ~~place~~ but in fact ~~one~~ has long since lost ~~one's~~ place.

which is always already both with and the violence of reading

Elfriede Jelinek. *Her Not All Her*, 19.

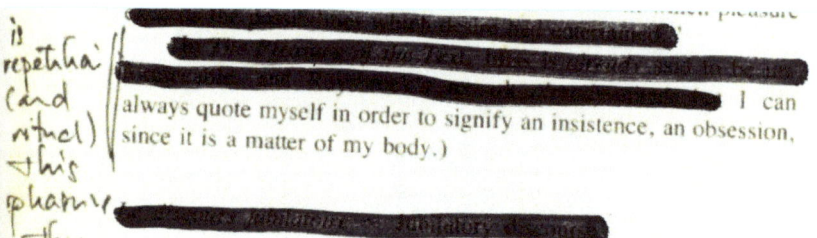

is repetition (and ritual) this pharmakon

I can always quote myself in order to signify an insistence, an obsession, since it is a matter of my body.)

Roland Barthes. *Roland Barthes*, 112.

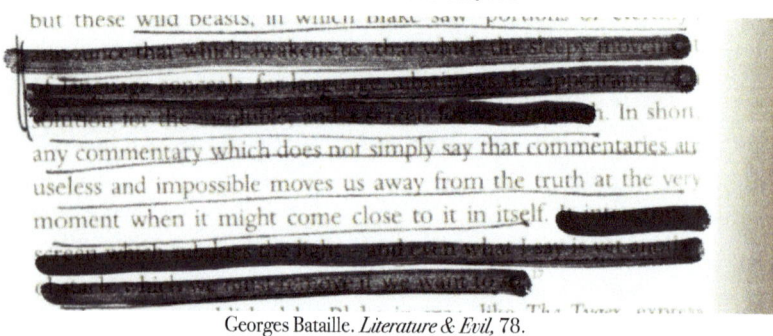

any commentary which does not simply say that commentaries are useless and impossible moves us away from the truth at the very moment when it might come close to it in itself.

Georges Bataille. *Literature & Evil*, 78.

and even what I say is yet another obstacle which we must remove if we want to *see*.

Ibid: 78

~~According to an initial vision, the image-repertoire is simple: it is the discourse of others *insofar as I see it* (I put it between quotation marks). Then I turn the scopia on myself: I see my language insofar as it is seen: I see it *naked* (without quotation marks): this is the disgraced, painful phase of the image-repertoire.~~
A third vision then appears: that of infinitely spread-out languages, of parentheses never to be closed: a utopian vision in that it supposes a mobile, plural reader, who nimbly inserts and removes the quotation marks: who begins to write *with me*.

161

who writes by responding to and with the text — and hears/(else) accepts responsibility — in this reading requires choosing /ethics.

Roland Barthes. *Roland Barthes*, 161.

Roland Barthes. *Empire of Signs*, translated by Richard Howard. New York: Hill & Day, 1983.

Faraway

If I want to imagine a fictive nation, I can give it an invented name, treat it declaratively as a novelistic object, ~~create a new Garabagne, so as to compromise no real country by my fantasy (though it is then that fantasy itself I compromise by the signs of literature)~~. I can also ~~— though in no way claiming to represent or to analyze reality itself (these being the major gestures of Western discourse) —~~ isolate somewhere in the world (*faraway*) a certain number of features <u>(a term employed in linguistics), and out of these features deliberately form a system.</u> It is this system which I shall call: Japan.

~~Hence Orient and Occident cannot be taken here as "realities" to be compared and contrasted historically, philosoph...~~

It is this system which I shall call:
Roland Barthes.

Music is always a stranger on this earth, but the disadvantage of language is that is can all too quickly seem familiar

– Elfriede Jelinek

Le Chapeau Invisibilité

Jachin Pousson

Pirouettes

> 146 Marguerite Duras
>
> We never know who the voices are. But just by the way each of them has forgotten or remembers, we get to know them more deeply than through their identity. ~~The story is a love story immobilized in the culmination of passion. Around it is another story, a story of horror — famine and leprosy mingled in the pestilential humidity of the monsoon — which is also immobilized in a daily paroxysm.~~
>
> The woman, Anne-Marie S...

Marguerite Duras. *India Song*, translated by Barbara Bray. New York: Grove Press, 1994: 146.

To speak.

Perhaps, one is tempted to say, perchance to dream. But then, one would have to ask, we would have to ask — for, there were always two whenever speaking is involved, even if one is speaking with oneself — *what one is dreaming of.*

Or, even: *who is one dreaming of?*

But perhaps all speech is a dream. Or, at least: one has to first dream in order to speak, at least with another. Not necessarily that *my dream is yours* — for, there is neither need, nor reason, that the two are having the same dream — but that the two in conversation are actually speaking, have the possibility of speaking, with each other. So perhaps, not a need for the same dream, but that they dream of the same. Even if the same is the fact that not only is one dreaming, but that the other is having a dream — that there is another dream.

A dream of another.

And in that dream, whilst dreaming, awaken themselves to the possibility of another. Even if the other, the possibility of speaking with another, remains within, remains only but, a dream.

Never forgetting that even as one wakes (*se réveiller*), one might still hear echoes of a, your, dream (*rêve*); that even whilst awake, one might still be in a dream.

Thus, to speak is always already to speak *with*. But even as speaking is a relationality, even as there is always another in that speaking, one should never forget — or, at least, attempt to remember — that "we never know who the voices are." Perhaps then, speaking with is nothing more than an attempt to hear another's memories — memories that are always also haunted by forgetting, that bring with it forgetting as they are recalled, as they recall. Not that this hearing will allow one to know another, or even open another to one, but that one might perhaps catch a glimpse — if one can even say that of hearing — of them. However, this would be a sight of a sound — or, sound of a sight — beyond "who the voices are," perhaps even outside the voices themselves.

Perhaps then, this is the dream: knowing the other that is with another.

Where to speak is not just speaking with another, but also with their other.

Where perhaps, their other is the very site — the condition of the possibility — of speaking itself.

* * *

How then can one, I, have a conversation with Roland Barthes?

A question which opens the question of whether I am possibly misreading him. Even as I am attempting to read him, attend to his thought. Perhaps particularly as I am trying to do so. After all, each attempt, each time one tries, *chaque essai*, is always also an assailing: where trying to read a work is also trying a work, putting it on trial; bringing it not just before the law, but perhaps one's own law. For, we should try not to forget Kant's reminder that there is no possible rationality, reason, to judgment: one judges only at the moment of judging. Which also suggests that not only does one not know how one is judging before doing so, one might not even know when or even if one is judging. So, not just that one judges secretly, not just that one's judgement might always remain secret from one, but that the fact that one is judging, that one is a judge, might always remain hidden from one.

Thus, each time, even as, one judges, the judgment is indivorceable from a judgment of whether one is a judge.

And, perhaps here, it might be time to attend to the register that to converse is to live with, to turn about (*vertere*) with (*con*). Keeping in mind that being in a relationality, conversing with, does not necessarily mean agreement: for, to converse is also to be the exact opposite. Thus, to be with whilst also possibly turning around (*conversus*), turning about (*convertere*). However, this is a disagreement that still maintains the relation, that still agrees to be with, even as both are turning, moving around. That even as there might be divergences, even as one is momentarily turned away from – or even against – the other (*versus*), there is always already the openness to the possibility of changing one's mind, one's position, an openness to the possibility of conversion, being converted.

But, since any genuine attempt at being with another involves acknowledging the otherness of the other, this suggests: not only is the sole aspect of the relationship that might be open to one's knowledge, one's judgement, oneself, the only known conversion — at least the only one that can be judged to have occurred — is that of one's self.

Which also suggests that even as I am attempting to have a conversation with Roland Barthes, a conversation based on sight, on seeing what is in front of me — speaking with Barthes through his text, through reading him — I can never quite be sure not only if I am misreading him, nor if the conversation is only me turning around myself, but that it is only because of the possibility of its exact opposite that one is able to converse. For, it is only because of the potential disagreement, dissention, dissensus even, that the possibility of relationality is maintained: otherwise, both would be the same and not only difference but the very relationality itself would collapse. Thus, if one allows for the possibility that reading Barthes is an attempt to converse with him, it is premised on the potential misreading of the text, of his text.

Perhaps even: without the possibility of misreading, there cannot be reading.

For, if reading is the relationality between one and the text where the text remains wholly other from oneself, this suggests that for this relationship to continue, grow, move, it must never quite complete itself. Thus, each time reading occurs – if reading can be said to happen, to be an act – it not only brings with it potential misreading(s), but that misreading is both the limit and condition of reading itself.

Which means that conversation not only requires a turning around – opposition, reverses, reversals, movements, flows – but always also its converse, in the precise sense of a non-conversation. Speaking not just through, or even by, silence, but by a non-speaking: where each moment of speech, of speaking with, is always also a non-speaking.

Where perhaps the two are not quite distinguishable.

Where the difference between speaking and non-speaking, between conversation and its converse, is a matter of judgment.

Which also means that the possibility of a conversation is always already fraught with, brings with it, its *non-*; keeping in mind that

the dash, the line between the conversation and
its negation, is a link that separates as it brings
together, that might also dash, break apart, even
as it joins.

Thus, any conversation requires a conversion,
first needs one to be converted to its
possibility – for, even as there is more than
one in any conversation, both ones, all ones,
in the relationality, have to make this decision
independently, wholly singularly.

Where one has to take a leap of faith …

Even, perhaps especially, when the conversation
                        lies in the text between the two.

For, even as the text is what brings the two
together, puts the two in communication
– in communion even – it is what connects
as it separates, brings together whilst never
ceasing to remind the two that they are distinct.
And the moment the bridge is bridged, what
collapses is none other than the possibility
of communication – what is sundered is
relationality itself.

Which means that, since one can only know
what one reads, one sees, one speaks – for,
even if there is a response, this has to be heard,
read, seen, through one – in order to maintain
this gap between, the gap which is the very
condition of relationality, one has to hold on

to the possibility that one's reading, speech, understanding even, brings with it its converse; whether it is there or not is perhaps somewhat irrelevant.

Perhaps then, the conversation is both in the text – what is in front of one – and what is not at the same time. Not that we can quite know what, or where, this *not-* is; even as we posit that the *not-* might well be part of the text itself.

Perhaps then, in any conversation, the space where, in which, it takes place, is both at and also converse to its very site. Thus, even as one attempts – we, I, attempt – to read Roland Barthes' text carefully, attend to his words, one must also keep in mind Bertolt Brecht's warning that

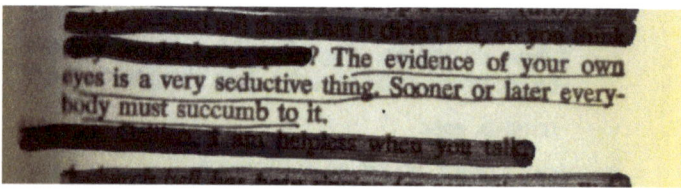

Bertolt Brecht. *Galileo,* edited, with an introduction, by Eric Bentley & translated by Charles Laughton. New York: Grove Press, 1994: Act I, sc iii, 63

That what lies in front of one, seemingly for one to take in, inhabit, make part of one's *habitus*, repeat, mimic, learn, know, might not be just lying down there, just in front of one, but might well be bringing itself before one, presenting itself, bringing forth, writing itself onto one — in ways that are, perhaps will always remain, unknown to one. Never forgetting that one is — I am — reading, conversing with, Brecht's text even as I am attempting to heed his warning, even as I am reading his text as a warning. That there is no possibility of heeding his warning without first reading him, the text, the site without which the conversation cannot even begin. Thus, even as every conversation requires the possibility of its converse, even as the conversation might be both within and beyond its site at the same time, the site of the conversation is part of the conversation itself: not just as its space, the venue where it occurs, but that it is the necessary condition of being with, the very possibility of the *con* itself — even as there is no place without the coming together, relationality, that is the conversation. Perhaps then, the site only comes into being when there is a coming together — perhaps even a coming with (*con*) at the point of the turn (*vertere*).

And what else is a coming together at a turn than a *trope* — perhaps not just a turn of speech, but that there is *speech only at a turn*.

And here, if we pay attention, we might be able hear the possibility of being conned whenever one is being with, when there is, an other; a turn of speech turning tricks, as it were. For, just because one recognises that it "is a very seductive thing," even if one attempts to put up

> You realise the sun doesn't go down
> It's just an illusion caused by
> the world spinning round.
>
> — The Flaming Lips

one's guard, it is not as if one can do anything about it – resistance is somewhat futile.

For, even as
 one is still seduced by sunsets.

That is, after all, the risk of attending to another, of hospitality, of opening oneself to the possibility of another, of communication – of conversation itself.

That is, perhaps, the risk of dreaming of the possibility of *conversing with*: after all, it is hardly inconceivable that one might con oneself, just be conning oneself, into spinning right round, baby right round.

* * *

Est-ce le jeu que nous jouons lorsque nous lisons?

For, one should never forget that there are rules.

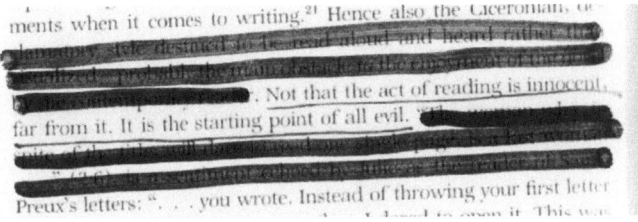

Paul de Man. *Allegories of Reading: Figural Language in Rousseau, Nietzsche, Rilke, and Proust.* New Haven: Yale University Press, 1979: 194.

Even as Paul de Man might entreat us to think of the possibility that reading is the beginning of all evil, that reading is the opening of questions – some of which might never be answered, might never be answerable – one should keep in mind that it is always also governed by not only the law of grammar – for, one can always subvert laws, transgress them – but by the rule of meaning itself. Where the unwritten, unspoken, rule is that when one reads, one should derive a meaning – not necessarily semantic, but at least a sense of sense, *un sens du sens*.

However, the trouble with rules is that there is no possibility of negotiation: one either plays by them or leaves. And what makes the rule even more iron clad is the fact that it is unwritten, unspoken; thus, there is nothing that one can resist against, there is nothing against which one can mount any resistance. In fact, since it is never laid out in front of one, it might well be that even as one is attempting to resist — especially if one is trying to transgress — one is doing nothing more than writing, speaking, this very rule, these very rules, into existence. Perhaps then, the question should be — even as the first question, *is this the game we play as we read?*, continues to echo in the background — *how do we read the game as we play?*

> *Comment pouvons-nous lire le jeu pendant que nous jouons ?*

And once the relationship between reading and playing is opened — not just through the game, but where the game is the very object of reading and play — there is always also the possibility that the rule itself can be played with, read. Not in the sense of resisting, breaking, but perhaps, by attending to the rule, by reading it extremely carefully, one might be able to allow it to limit itself.

For, since there is the possibility that it is one who is erecting, enacting, these rules, then perhaps the harsher the rule — the more obvious it is — the greater the possibility that it slips into the realm of the law, the greater one's possibility of playing with it. After all, one should bear in mind — to echo St. Paul — the notion that every law brings with it, brings about, its own transgression.

Perhaps then, one of our strategies of defense is to cite, writing though citations – scare quotes. For, even as they are homages, attempts to credit the place where, person from whom, one's thoughts come, are a nod to the history of an idea, they also a way of building a shield, marshalling one's sources, around oneself: as if to say, *if you don't like this notion, if you don't agree with me, take it up with the one who wrote it, take it up with Roland Barthes*. And here, one should never forget that when one cites, not only is it always already out of context – and thus, an act of terror on a text – one is also summoning the text, perhaps even its author, to stand before one; handing out a citation, as it were.

But, *who comes?*

For, it is not as if the one who writes can be there – or, at least, it is not as if the one who writes can always be there. And even if (s)he is beside one as the summons is being made, at the point one issues the summons, (s)he can only respond after the fact: *what one has said, one has said*; *what I have written, I have written*. Perhaps then, a citation, citing him, only makes too clear that (s)he is not there, no longer there, perhaps was never quite there.

[Perhaps then, all citations are, citing is, a preparation for the absence – death? *death of a writer; what does that even mean? can a writer actually die; if a writer is a writer because of his writing, once written can (s)he actually be dead? but, if (s)he is a writer because of writing, and writing is of the order of the dead, can (s)he ever have been separate from that realm?* – of not just the author, but even the writer, the one who writes, the one who has written.]

But, it is not as if there is absolutely nothing, no one, there, as well. For, even if the writer is absent in his writing, his writing remains: the mark that (s)he makes is indelible; without which, there is no possibility of reading. However, the moment it is read, the moment one reads his writing, it may no longer have anything to do with his writing, with him. Not because one is free to read in whatever way one wants to, that pleases one — we should never forget that there are rules — but that the inscription not only precedes the reading, but also quite possibly remains beyond all reading(s). For, even as the mark of writing has to come before reading, the mark can only be known through reading: thus, all we can have is the read mark, the mark that is read. The mark that is writing — the mark of writing itself — might well always both be beyond us and is what remains, is both before and after.

Où, elle est avant — et après — la lettre.

Perhaps then, the question is: *what comes?*

For, something certainly comes to us as we read: even if we do not comprehend what it is that comes. There is undeniably a semantic meaning — a signification. There is almost surely always also an effect, a manner in which it affects us — a significance. But what if there is perhaps something more — or less, since we do not know what it is.

> What if, in the moment of the turn, the *pirouette*, there is the *coming with as a turn*?

Not that the *coming with* and *turn* are the same, but that as one turns — at least in that moment of turning — there is a possible *coming with*: a *coming with as the turn happens*, but a *with* where *coming* and the *turn* are always still separate from each other.

> *Con — vertere.*

&, perhaps always also,
> *turning — with.*

Perhaps here, one could open the possibility that *the what that comes to us* is a sense? Not just phenomenologically, for that would still suggest an *a priori* code, and thus be semantically decoded, or at least decodable; but as a *feeling*, one prior to, before, any identification or signification, one that came to one, from beyond one, perhaps in ways that remain unknowable to one – a sense before any sense, *un sens avant la possibilité du sens*, a feeling that there might be a feeling, as it were.

But, since one is – I am – the one who feels, this suggests that the moment one senses, or thinks one feels, one has always also closed the possibility of a something more. Sensing as the end of feeling – feeling as the end of senses.

After all, it is not as if one can quite understand understanding.

Jacques Rancière. *The Ignorant Schoolmaster: Five Lessons in Emancipation*, translated, with an introduction, by Kristin Ross. Stanford: Stanford University Press, 1991: 63-64.

Perhaps then, the something more, possibilities — even the coming together that is in communion, communication, community — is then only potentially glimpsed as it flickers in the turn. Once grasped — once someone makes a claim to knowing, to understanding — it disappears.

Of course, one can object and point out that in stating the very limits to knowing, to understanding, in positing the possibility that potentially lies in a turning that comes, I am also falling into the same trap of claiming to know something that cannot be known, that I claim cannot be known.

And that might perhaps be true.

However, here — echoing Roland Barthes — I might plead with you to try not to forget that I am not making truth claims. For, "it must all be considered as if spoken by a character in a novel — or by several characters." Which is not to say that stories are unimportant — far from it. But that their importance lies not so much in their claims, but that they are retold, that they are reimagined, repeated imaginatively — always the same, that is always already different — that generate their own tales in their tellings.

For, one should never forget that to speak of possibilities — in this case, to attempt to imagine the possibility of reading as conversation, coming together, community even — is to speak of the *as-yet-unknown*. And perhaps, the always unknowable. For, there is no reason to believe that it may not remain always-to-come. Or that, since we know not what it is, it has already come but continues to remain beyond us.

Thus, our attempts to converse with conversation, commune with community, are always also an attempt to speak with, think with, perhaps even be with, turn with, an absence, an absence that might well be absolute. A speech that is only possible if we open — if one imagines, reads, writes, narrates, opens — the possibility of speaking with one we know not of, perhaps cannot, never can, know of.

Perhaps then, conversation itself — after all, one can only catch a glimpse of *who* or *what* one is turning with after the turning happens — is premised on the possibility of turning with what, one who, is, and might always remain, unknowable to one.

Where the necessary condition of conversation is the possibility of speaking with death.

* * *

... and as we are having this conversation, as I am speaking with — perhaps, even to — you, as you are listening to me, I wonder if it is even possible to speak of death, not to mention speak to Death.

Herself? Himself? Itself?

For, even as we spend quite a lot of our time telling tales of death, of deaths, about death, about deaths that are not quite just deaths, we are merely making utterances about death, perhaps even describing deaths, but are never really quite able to say what death is.

Let alone who.

Which opens the question: does one speak of *death,* or *the idea of death?* Keeping in mind that death — or Death, if you prefer proper names — remains beyond us. One only experiences death; and as far as I can tell, no one has come back to tell us whom we face, we are facing. Or, whom one is facing: for, perhaps one always faces death alone.
        Even the Nazarene.

All he did was: announce his resurrection, tell us that *to conquer death, you only have to die*. But, he didn't bother to tell us exactly whom — or what — he conquered. Which, in itself, is no reason to doubt his words, his claim. Perhaps he did overcome the idea of death — and only left

its, his, her, effects untouched. After all, the last
I checked, people were still affected, still dying.
For which I am — morbid, as it may sound —
strangely thankful. That way, at least I know I am
speaking with you.

Or, at least the possibility of you.

But, which you? For, one should try not to
forget that everyone dies twice: once bodily,
again when one is forgotten — not necessarily
in that order, nor even at separate times. Which
might also mean that there are two; there is
more than one, you. That speaking with one
involves the death of the other, all others. And
that, since I am — or at least attempting to —
speak with Death, this mean that even the un-
dead Death must also be dead.

Thus, I can only be speaking with you in
memory of you.

For, even as I call you Death, even as I personify
you, my only access to you is through your
name; I can only attempt to speak of you, to
you, imaginatively. And here, one should bear
in mind that imagination springs from memory:
for, to imagine something, to have an inkling
of it, one has to first know of it. But, of death,
I know nothing except its effects. And yet, we
continue to speak of death, I continue to speak
of death, you continue to listen to me speak
about death.

Thus, speaking the unspeakable.

Or, perhaps: speaking of a memory that I have yet to have. And, since death is quite possibly a memory to come – even if it has never left my side – perhaps then, the only way I can know of this is if I, we, have always already been dead. And are only waiting for our bodies to catch up with this memory, this memory of the unknown.

Perhaps, that is the only way I can be speaking to you of death. Even as I know not what I am speaking of.

By speaking of death as it speaks through me.

Speaking to you as you speak through me.

I'll be your mirror ...

He tried not to be vain, but he was happy about the idea of becoming famous.

- Silvina Ocampo

It is somewhat difficult to sit, on a chair, watching someone sketch you. Watch someone watch you; as a sketching – ostensibly of you – appears on a sheet of paper. On a sheet that remains out of view; that fills up beyond you, is filled up with you – whilst it remains veiled from you.

Marked with you.
Where every stroke, line, trace, is a mark of you. A mark that marks nothing but the fact that you were no longer there. That you never actually needed to be there.

Even as the site is increasingly filled with you.

For all sketching is done in blindness.

Where, at the point the stroke is made, (s)he has
to either look at the sheet and not at you, or you
and not the space which you allegedly fill.
An act of memory; always already haunted by
forgetting.
Of imagination; memory with forgetting quite
possibly written into it.
In preparation for nothing other than your
absence.

Preparing for your absence – with another.
Or: preparing your other for your absence.

An other who watches you watch.
Even as you cannot see it.
That you know – or perhaps hope – is looking
back at you.

***

Portraits;
traced (*traire*). Perhaps dragged,
pulled (*trahere*), forth (*por*).
Drawn out, dragged.
Lines – nothing other than traces,
tracks (*tractus*).

Mirrors: no one has ever knowingly described you in your essence ...
– Rainer Maria Rilke

Jeremy Fernando is the Jean Baudrillard Fellow at the European Graduate School, where he is also a Reader in Contemporary Literature & Thought. He works in the intersections of literature, philosophy, and the media; and has written eleven books — including *Reading Blindly, Living with Art, and Writing Death*. His work has been featured in magazines and journals such as *Berfrois, CTheory, TimeOut,* and *VICE*, amongst others; and he has been translated into Spanish and Slovenian. Exploring other media has led him to film, music, and art; and his work has been exhibited in Seoul, Vienna, Hong Kong, and Singapore. He is the editor of the thematic magazine *One Imperative*; and a Fellow of Tembusu College at the National University of Singapore.

Lim Lee Ching teaches interdisciplinary subjects at SIM University, Singapore. He is the editor of the *Singapore Review of Books*.

Jachin Pousson is an American musician, composer, and sound designer, currently living in Riga, Latvia. He began performing in Singapore as a drummer and lyricist, leading to numerous international festival and showcase appearances over a 5-year stretch. Simultaneously he participated in humanitarian efforts in Asia, Africa, and Eastern Europe, where he often took on the additional role of documenting the work in writing, film, photography, or sound recording, making many personal recordings of his own. Subsequently he moved to Copenhagen for a conservatory education in music composition at the Royal Danish Academy of Music in 2010. Drawn to the musical aesthetic of the Baltics, he later moved to Latvia and completed his Masters studies in composition at Jazep Vitols Latvian Music Academy in 2015. At present he remains an active musician and composer in Riga, in both the academic and electro-acoustic scenes.

Yanyun Chen draws, and is driven by questions. Her practice is rooted in the craft and the silent contemplation of making drawings. These drawings were exhibited in group shows in Singapore, notably ChanHampe Galleries, Artistry, and NoiseSingapore.

She is a Ph.D. candidate at the European Graduate School, where she completed her M.A. in Communications. She also received the Lee Kuan Yew Gold Medal Award and the Nanyang Scholarship for her undergraduate degree in animation from the School of Art, Design and Media, Nanyang Technological University, Singapore (first class honours). She has been trained at the Florence Academy of Art (FAA) in Sweden, The Animation Workshop in Denmark, and under puppet makers Miroslav Trejtnar and Zdar Sorm in the Czech Republic. She was an artist-in-residence at Hackerspace Singapore, and Tembusu College, at the National University of Singapore.

www.ingramcontent.com/pod-product-compliance
Lightning Source LLC
Chambersburg PA
CBHW042329150426
43193CB00005B/58